COLE PORTER
100ᵀᴴ ANNIVERSARY

Cover Illustration: Archie Williamson

CONTENTS

CONTENTS

Special thanks to ROBERT KIMBALL for his introduction,
and for his permission to print historical background
information from his book THE COMPLETE LYRICS OF COLE PORTER.

FOREWORD

This comprehensive collection of songs by Cole Porter is a splendid 100th birthday tribute to the artist regarded by many as the most sophisticated of America's composer-lyricists. Porter's association with Warner/Chappell began in 1919 and continued into the age of television and rock and roll when he ended his fabulous career.

He was born on June 9, 1891 in Peru, Indiana of a well-to-do family. Yet success did not come quickly or easily, and for all his precocity and skill (as a member of the Yale College Class of 1913, he wrote two of the school's most famous football songs, "Bull Dog" and "Bingo, Eli Yale"), he was dogged by a series of setbacks that delayed his rise to the top of his profession until the late 1920's.

The turning point in his career came through his friendship with Irving Berlin. In 1927, Berlin had suggested to producer B. Ray Goetz, Berlin's brother-in-law from his first marriage, that Goetz find Porter on the Lido in Venice (Porter lived for part of several years in Venice during the 1920's) and persuade him to write some American songs with a French flavor for Goetz' new show. Porter later said he fell on Goetz "like an over-eager puppy." The result was Porter's first big hit, PARIS, which included such songs as "Let's Do It (Let's Fall In Love)" and "Let's Misbehave," which are the earliest songs in this collection. PARIS premiered at Irving Berlin's Music Box Theatre on Broadway in 1928 with Mrs. Goetz — the great Gallic charmer Irene Bordoni — in the starring role.

By decade's end, as post World War I energy turned into frenzy, stock speculations went sour·and the widespread notion that Utopia had a price tag was discredited by the Crash of 1929 and all that followed, Porter's songs were a heady tonic for a disillusioned age. When America was in the depths of the Great Depression of the 1930's — Porter's most productive decade — his was a message of civilized cheer.

Even after the riding accident that crushed both his legs when a horse fell on him one October weekend in 1937, Porter continued to write his amusing, exhilarating, often poignant songs. Despite more than 30 operations over the years, and constant pain for the rest of his life, his courage remained enormous, his spirit indomitable, and his creative skill unimpaired. He finally lost the will to write, however, after the amputation of his right leg in 1958. He died in Santa Monica, California, on October 15, 1964.

Now, more than 25 years after his death, his work is more admired than ever. We honor him for his extraordinary legacy. He challenged our intelligence, chronicled our foibles, and made us laugh and cry as he touched our hearts.

— Robert Kimball, editor of COLE (1971) and THE COMPLETE LYRICS OF COLE PORTER (1983)

LET'S MISBEHAVE

From "Paris"

Words and Music by
COLE PORTER

You could have a great car - eer,__ And you should.__

On - ly one__ thing stops you, dear,__ You're too good.__

7

LET'S DO IT (Let's Fall In Love)
From "Paris"

Words and Music by
COLE PORTER

Refrain

1 Birds do it,— Bees do it,— E - ven ed - u - cat - ed
2 Spon - ges, they say, do it,— Oy - sters, down in Oy - ster

fleas do it,— Let's do it,— Let's fall in love.
Bay, do it,— Let's do it,— Let's fall in love.

— In Spain, the best up - per sets do it,—
— Cold Cape Cod clams, 'gainst their wish, do it,—

LET'S DO IT, LET'S FALL IN LOVE

Published October 1928. It replaced "Let's Misbehave" before the New York opening and was used later in the English production of the revue *Wake Up and Dream* (1929). The opening lines of refrain 1 were changed to the familiar "Birds do it, bees do it," etc., when Porter realized that many would find the words "Chinks" and "Japs" offensive. Introduced by Irene Bordoni and Arthur Margetson.

VERSE

When the little bluebird,
Who has never said a word,
Starts to sing "Spring, spring,"
When the little bluebell,
In the bottom of the dell,
Starts to ring "Ding, ding,"
When the little blue clerk,
In the middle of his work,
Starts a tune to the moon up above,
It is nature, that's all,
Simply telling us to fall
In love.

REFRAIN 1

And that's why Chinks do it, Japs do it,
Up in Lapland, little Lapps do it,
Let's do it, let's fall in love.
In Spain, the best upper sets do it,
Lithuanians and Letts do it,
Let's do it, let's fall in love.
The Dutch in old Amsterdam do it,
Not to mention the Finns,
Folks in Siam do it,
Think of Siamese twins.
Some Argentines, without means, do it,
People say, in Boston, even beans do it,
Let's do it, let's fall in love.

REFRAIN 2

The nightingales, in the dark do it,
Larks, k-razy for a lark, do it,
Let's do it, let's fall in love.
Canaries, caged in the house, do it,
When they're out of season, grouse do it,
Let's do it, let's fall in love.
The most sedate barnyard fowls do it,
When a chanticleer cries,
High-browed old owls do it,
They're supposed to be wise,
Penguins in flocks, on the rocks, do it,
Even little cuckoos, in their clocks, do it,
Let's do it, let's fall in love.

REFRAIN 3

Romantic sponges, they say, do it,
Oysters, down in Oyster Bay, do it,
Let's do it, let's fall in love.
Cold Cape Cod clams, 'gainst their wish, do it,
Even lazy jellyfish do it,
Let's do it, let's fall in love.
Electric eels, I might add, do it,
Though it shocks 'em, I know.
Why ask if shad do it?
Waiter, bring me shad roe.
In shallow shoals, English soles do it,
Goldfish, in the privacy of bowls, do it,
Let's do it, let's fall in love.

REFRAIN 3 (ENGLISH PRODUCTION)

Young whelks and winkles, in pubs, do it,
Little sponges, in their tubs, do it.
Let's do it, let's fall in love.
Cold salmon, quite 'gainst their wish, do it,
Even lazy jellyfish do it,
Let's do it, let's fall in love.
The most select schools of cod do it,
Though it shocks 'em, I fear,
Sturgeon, thank God, do it,
Have some caviar, dear.
In shady shoals, English soles do it,
Goldfish, in the privacy of bowls, do it,
Let's do it, let's fall in love.

REFRAIN 4

The dragonflies, in the reeds, do it,
Sentimental centipedes do it,
Let's do it, let's fall in love.
Mosquitoes, heaven forbid, do it,
So does ev'ry katydid, do it,
Let's do it, let's fall in love.
The most refined lady bugs do it,
When a gentleman calls,
Moths in your rugs, do it,
What's the use of moth balls?
Locusts in trees do it, bees do it,
Even overeducated fleas do it,
Let's do it, let's fall in love.

REFRAIN 5

The chimpanzees, in the zoos, do it,
Some courageous kangaroos do it,
Let's do it, let's fall in love.
I'm sure giraffes, on the sly, do it,
Heavy hippopotami do it,
Let's do it, let's fall in love.
Old sloths who hang down from twigs do it,
Though the efford is great,
Sweet guinea pigs do it,
Buy a couple and wait.
The world admits bears in pits do it,
Even pekineses in the Ritz, do it,
Let's do it, let's fall in love.

WHAT IS THIS THING CALLED LOVE?
From "Wake Up And Dream"

Words and Music by
COLE PORTER

Moderato

I was a hum-drum per-son, Lead-ing a life a
You gave me days of sun-shine, You gave me nights of

part, When love flew in through my win-dow wide And
cheer, You made my life an en-chant-ed dream, Till

18

AGUA SINCOPADA
From "Wake Up And Dream"

By
COLE PORTER

23

Tempo I.
Very staccato.

YOU DO SOMETHING TO ME
From "Fifty Million Frenchmen"

Words and Music by
COLE PORTER

And I gazed at you. Won't you tell me,

dear, Why, when you ap - pear, Some-thing hap-pens

to me And the strang-est feel - ing goes through me?

Slowly, with expression

Refrain

You do some-thing to me.

YOU DO SOMETHING TO ME

Published November 1929. *Frenchmen's* most famous song was introduced by Genevieve Tobin and William Gaxton.

VERSE 1

I was mighty blue,
Thought my life was through,
Till the heavens opened,
And I gazed at you.
Won't you tell me, dear,
Why, when you appear,
Something happens to me
And the strangest feeling goes through me?

REFRAIN

You do something to me,
Something that simply mystifies me.
Tell me, why should it be
You have the pow'r to hypnotize me?
Let me live 'neath your spell,
Do do that voodoo that you do so well,
For you do something to me
That nobody else could do.

VERSE 2

If I seem to stray
When you talk this way
It's because I'm wondering
What I ought to say.
I could cry, please don't,
But I believe I won't,
For when you talk to me
Such a soothing feeling goes through me.

THE TALE OF THE OYSTER

Published in *The Unpublished Cole Porter*. Added to *Frenchmen* before the New York opening to give comedienne Helen Broderick another song. An earlier version with a different lyric was called "The Scampi". After amusing the Venice social set, the lyric was rewritten, and the song, after first nearly going into *Wake Up and Dream,* had a brief life in *Frenchmen*. When *Frenchmen* opened in New York, some people, including the noted critic Gilbert Seldes, found the song offensive. The program for the week of January 6, 1930, shows that "The Tale of the Oyster" (listed in the program as "The Tale of an Oyster") had been deleted from the show.

The song was rescued from oblivion by Ben Bagley and recorded by Kaye Ballard on Bagley's *Cole Porter Revisited* album.

Down by the sea lived a lonesome oyster,
Ev'ry day getting sadder and moister.
He found his home life awf'lly wet,
And longed to travel with the upper set.
Poor little oyster.
Fate was kind to that oyster we know,
When one day the chef from the Park Casino
Saw that oyster lying there,
And said, "I'll put you on my bill of fare."
Lucky little oyster.
See him on his silver platter,
Watching the queens of fashion chatter.
Hearing the wives of millionaires
Discuss their marriages and their love affairs.
Thrilled little oyster.
See that bivalve social climber
Feeding the rich Mrs. Hoggenheimer,
Think of his joy as he gaily glides
Down to the middle of her gilded insides.
Proud little oyster.
After lunch Mrs. H. complains,
And says to her hostess, "I've got such pains.
I came to town on my yacht today,
But I think I'd better hurry back to Oyster Bay."
Scared little oyster.
Off they go thru the troubled tide,
The yacht rolling madly from side to side.
They're tossed about till that poor young oyster
Finds that it's time he should quit his cloister.
Up comes the oyster.
Back once more where he started from.
He murmured, "I haven't a single qualm,
For I've had a taste of society
And society has had a taste of me."
Wise little oyster.

THE TALE OF THE OYSTER
From "Fifty Million Frenchmen"

Words and Music by
COLE PORTER

34

FIND ME A PRIMITIVE MAN
From "Fifty Million Frenchmen"

Words and Music by
COLE PORTER

REFRAIN

FIND ME ___ A PRIM-I-TIVE MAN ___ Built on ___

a prim-i-tive plan; ___ Some one ___ with

vig-or and vim, ___ I don't mean the kind that be-longs to a club, But the

kind that has a club that be-longs to him, I could be ___ the per-son-al slave ___

YOU'VE GOT THAT THING

Published December 1929. A manuscript found at Tams-Witmark included the lyric for the previously unknown third refrain. Introduced by Jack Thompson and Betty Compton.

VERSE

Since first you blew in like a boisterous breeze
I often have wondered, dear,
Why gentlemen all seem to fall on their knees
The moment that you appear?
Your fetching physique is hardly unique,
You're mentally not so hot;
You'll never win laurels because of your morals,
But I'll tell you what you've got

REFRAIN 1

You've got that thing, you've got that thing,
That thing that makes birds forget to sing.
Yes, you've got that thing, that certain thing.
You've got that charm, that subtle charm
That makes young farmers desert the farm,
'Cause you've got that thing, that certain thing.
You've got what Adam craved when he
With love for Eve was tortured,
She only had an apple tree,
But you, you've got an orchard.
You've got those ways, those taking ways
That make me rush off to Cartier's
For a wedding ring,
You've got that thing.

REFRAIN 2

You've got that thing, you've got that thing,
That thing that makes vines prefer to cling.
Yes, you've got that thing, that certain thing.
You've got those looks, those fatal looks.
That make book censors enjoy their books,
'Cause you've got that thing, that certain thing.
Just what made Samson be, for years,
Delilah's lord and keeper?
She only had a pair of shears.
But you, you've got a reaper.
You've got that pow'r, that pow'r to grip
That make me map out a wedding trip
For the early spring,
You've got that thing.

REFRAIN 3

You've got that thing, you've got that thing,
That thing that makes bees refuse to sting.
Yes, you've got that thing, that certain thing.
You've got that kiss, that kiss that warms,
That makes reformers reform reforms,
'Cause you've got that thing, that certain thing.
They tell us Trojan Helen's lips
Made ev'ry man her slavey.
If her face launched a thousand ships
Well, yours could launch an navy.
You've got that love, and such a lot*
It makes me think you're prepared for what
Any stork might bring.
You've got that thing.

*You've ideas inside your head
That make me order an extra bed
With an extra spring.
You've got that thing.

YOU'VE GOT THAT THING
From "Fifty Million Frenchmen"

Words and Music by
COLE PORTER

Since first you blew in _ like a bois-ter-ous breeze _ I oft-en have won - dered, dear, _

_____ Why gen-tle-men all _ seem to fall on their knees _ The mo-ment that you _ ap-

pear? _____ Your fetch-ing phy-sique _ is hard-ly u - nique, _ You're

LOVE FOR SALE
From "The New Yorkers"

Words and Music by
COLE PORTER

When the on-ly sound in the

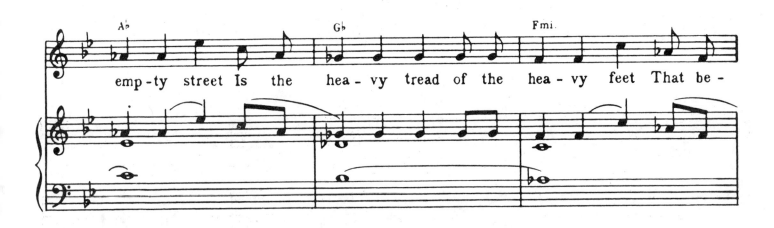

emp-ty street Is the hea-vy tread of the hea-vy feet That be-

long to a lone-some cop, I _____ o - pen

I HAPPEN TO LIKE NEW YORK

From "The New Yorker"

Words and Music by
COLE PORTER

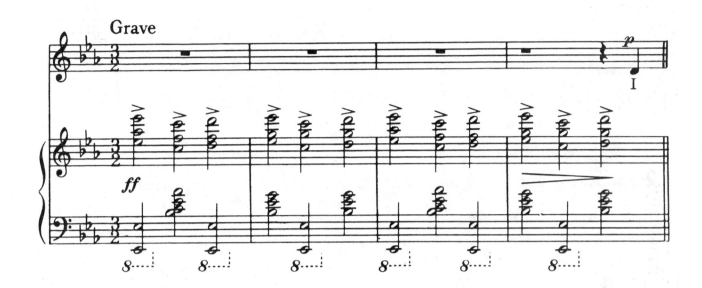

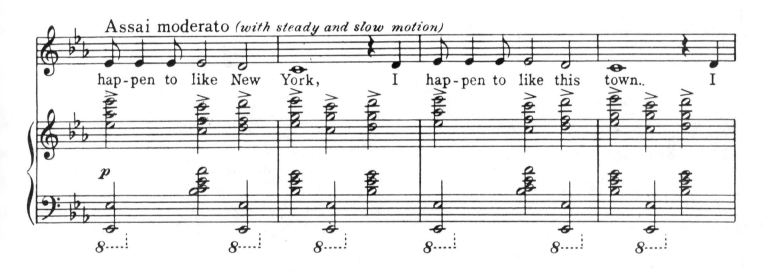

hap-pen to like New York, I hap-pen to like this town. I

like the cit-y air, I like to drink of it, The more I know New York the

NIGHT AND DAY

From "The Gay Divorce"

Words and Music by
COLE PORTER
French Version By
Emélia Renaud

AFTER YOU
From "The Gay Divorce"

Words and Music by
COLE PORTER

MISTER AND MISSUS FITCH
From "The Gay Divorce"

Words and Music by
COLE PORTER

66

THE PHYSICIAN

Published September 1933. Originally titled "But He Never Says He Loves Me," it was first presented in the pre-New York performances of *The New Yorkers* (1930). Subsequently, it was earmarked for the unproduced show *Star Dust* (1931). The title change to "The Physician" and a few lyric changes occurred during rehearsals for *Nymph Errant*. Gertrude Lawrence, who introduced it, recorded it on October 18, 1933. Porter recorded it on January 3, 1935.

VERSE

Once I loved such a shattering physician,
Quite the best-looking doctor in the state.
He looked after my physical condition,
And his bedside manner was great.
When I'd gaze up and see him there above me,
Looking less like a doctor than a Turk,
I was tempted to whisper, "Do you love me,
Or do you merely love your work?"

REFRAIN 1

He said my bronchial tubes were entrancing,
My epiglottis filled him with glee,
He simply loved my larynx
And went wild about my pharynx,
But he never said he loved me.
He said my epidermis was darling,
And found my blood as blue as could be,
He went through wild ecstatics,
When I showed him my lymphatics,
But he never said he loved me.
And though, no doubt,
It was not very smart of me,
I kept on a-wracking my soul
To figure out
Why he loved ev'ry part of me,
And yet not me as a whole.
With my esophagus he was ravished,
Enthusiastic to a degree,
He said 'twas just enormous,
My appendix vermiformis,
But he never said he loved me.

REFRAIN 2

He said my cerebellum was brilliant,
And my cerebrum far from N.G.,
I know he thought a lotta
My medulla oblongata,
But he never said he loved me.
He said my maxillaries were marvels,
And found my sternum stunning to see,
He did a double hurdle
When I shook my pelvic girdle,
But he never said he loved me.
He seemed amused
When he first made a test of me
To further his medical art,
Yet he refused
When he'd fix up the rest of me,
To cure that ache in my heart.
I know he thought my pancreas perfect,
And for my spleen was keen as could be,
He said of all his sweeties,
I'd the sweetest diabetes,
But he never said he loved me.

REFRAIN 3

He said my vertebrae were "sehr schöne,"
And called my coccyx "plus que gentil,"
He murmured "molto bella,"
When I sat on his patella,
But he never said he loved me.
He took a fleeting look at my thorax,
And started singing slightly off key,
He cried, "May Heaven strike us,"
When I played my umbilicus,
But he never said he loved me.
As it was dark,
I suggested we walk about
Before he returned to his post.
Once in the park,
I induced him to talk about
The thing I wanted the most.
He lingered on with me until morning,
Yet when I tried to pay him his fee,
He said, "Why, don't be funny,
It is I who owe you money,"
But he never said he loved me.

THE PHYSICIAN (But He Never Said He Loved Me)
From "Nymph Errant"

Words and Music by
COLE PORTER

70

REFRAIN

IT'S BAD FOR ME

Published September 1933. Introduced by Gertrude Lawrence.

VERSE

Your words go through and through me
And leave me totally dazed,
For they do such strange things to me
They nearly make me gloomy,
For you, dear, are so clever,
So obviously "the top,"
I wish you'd go on forever,
I wish even more you'd stop.

REFRAIN

For it's bad for me, it's bad for me,
This knowledge that you're going mad for me,
I feel certain my friends would be glad for me,
But it's bad for me.
It's so good for me, so new for me,
To see someone in such a stew for me,
And when you say you'd do all you could for me
It's so good for me, it's bad for me.
I though I'd been, till you met me,
Completely put on the shelf,
But since you started to pet me
I'm just crazy about myself.
Oh, it's sweet for me, it's swell for me,
To know that you're going through hell for me,
Yet no matter however appealing
I still have a feeling
It's bad for me.

IT'S BAD FOR ME

From "Nymph Errant"

Words and Music by
COLE PORTER

EXPERIMENT

Published September 1933. Introduced by Moya Nugent; reprised by Gertrude Lawrence. Revised for the un-produced film *Mississippi Belle*, 1943-1944. Both versions appear here.

VERSE

Before you leave these portals
To meet less fortunate mortals,
There's just one final message
I would give to you.
You all have learned reliance
On the sacred teachings of science,
So I hope, through life, you never will decline
In spite of philistine
Defiance
To do what all good scientists do.

REFRAIN

Experiment.
Make it your motto day and night.
Experiment
And it will lead you to the light.
The apple on the top of the tree
Is never too high to achieve,
So take an example from Eve,
Experiment.
Be curious,
Though interfering friends may frown.
Get furious
At each attempt to hold you down.
If this advice you always employ
The future can offer you infinite joy
And merriment.
Experiment
And you'll see.

Revised version for the film MISSISSIPPI BELLE (1943-1944)

VERSE

As I was leaving high school
My pet professor of my school
Said: My dear, one parting message I would give
    to you.
By now you've learned reliance
On the sacred teaching of science,
So I hope, through life, you never will decline,
In spite of philistine
Defiance
To do what all good scientists do.

REFRAIN 1 (SAME AS ORIGINAL REFRAIN)

INTERLUDE

And now, each one of you, do
Let me adapt this ditty to you.

REFRAIN 2

Experiment.
Whenever doubtful take a chance.
Experiment
And you'll discover sweet romance.
When in a state of ignorant bliss
Regarding a creature you crave
'Tis folly, my friend, to behave,
Experiment,
Be curious,
And when you've picked a perfect wife,
Get furious
Till she is yours and yours for life.
If this you do (and no cock-and-bull)
In time she may give you a nurs'ry full*
Of merriment.
Experiment
And you'll see.

*Or:
The future may give you a nurs'ry full

EXPERIMENT
From "Nymph Errant"

Words and Music by
COLE PORTER

REFRAIN

I GET A KICK OUT OF YOU
From "Anything Goes"

Words and Music by
COLE PORTER

YOU'RE THE TOP
From "Anything Goes"

Words and Music by
COLE PORTER

At words po-et-ic I'm so pa-thet-ic that I

al-ways have found it best,____ In-stead of get-ting 'em off____ my

88

REFRAIN

90

YOU'RE THE TOP

VERSE 1

At words poetic, I'm so pathetic
That I always have found it best,
Instead of getting 'em off my chest,
To let 'em rest unexpressed.
I hate parading
My serenading,
As I'll probably miss a bar,
But if this ditty
Is not so pretty,
At least it'll tell you
How great you are.

REFRAIN 1

You're the top!
You're the Colosseum.
You're the top!
You're the Louvre Museum.
You're a melody from a symphony by Strauss,
You're a Bendel bonnet,
A Shakespeare sonnet,
You're Mickey Mouse.
You're the Nile,
You're the Tow'r of Pisa,
You're the smile
On the Mona Lisa.
I'm a worthless check, a total wreck, a flop,
But if, baby, I'm the bottom
You're the top!

VERSE 2

Your words poetic are not pathetic.
On the other hand, boy, you shine,
And I can feel after every line
A thrill divine
Down my spine.
Now gifted humans like Vincent Youmans
Might think that your song is bad,
But for a person who's just rehearsin'
Well, I gotta say this my lad:

REFRAIN 2

You're the top!
You're Mahatma Gandhi.
You're the top!
You're Napoleon brandy.
You're the purple light of a summer night in
  Spain.
You're the National Gall'ry,
You're Garbo's sal'ry,
You're cellophane.
You're sublime,
You're a turkey dinner,
You're the time
Of the Derby winner.
I'm a toy balloon that is fated soon to pop,
But if, baby, I'm the bottom
You're the top!

REFRAIN 3

You're the top!
You're a Ritz hot toddy.
You're the top!
You're a Brewster body.
You're the boats that glide on the sleepy Zuider
  Zee,
You're a Nathan panning,
You're Bishop Manning,
You're broccoli.
You're a prize,
You're a night at Coney.

You're the eyes
Of Irene Bordoni.
I'm a broken doll, a fol-de-rol, a blop,
But if, baby, I'm the bottom
You're the top!

REFRAIN 4

You're the top!
You're an Arrow collar.
You're the top!
You're a Coolidge dollar.
You're the nimble tread of the feet of Fred
  Astaire,
You're an O'Neill drama,
You're Whistler's mama,
You're Camembert.
You're a rose,
You're Inferno's Dante,
You're the nose
On the great Durante.
I'm just in the way, as the French would say
"De trop,"
But if, baby, I'm the bottom
You're the top.

REFRAIN 5

You're the top!
You're a Waldorf salad.
You're the top!
You're a Berlin ballad.
You're a baby grand of a lady and a gent,
You're an old Dutch master,
You're Mrs. Astor,
You're Pepsodent.
You're romance,
You're the steppes of Russia,
You're the pants on a Roxy usher.
I'm a lazy lout that's just about to stop,
But if, baby, I'm the bottom
You're the top!

REFRAIN 6

You're the top!
You're a dance in Bali.
You're the top!
You're a hot tamale.
You're an angel, you, simply too, too, too diveen,
You're a Botticelli,
You're Keats,
You're Shelley,
You're Ovaltine.
You're a boon,
You're the dam at Boulder,
You're the moon over Mae West's shoulder.
I'm a nominee of the G.O.P.
  or GOP,
But if, baby, I'm the bottom
You're the top!

REFRAIN 7

You're the top!
You're the Tower of Babel.
You're the top!
You're the Whitney Stable.
By the river Rhine,
You're a sturdy stein of beer,
You're a dress from Saks's,
You're next year's taxes,
You're stratosphere.
You're my thoist,
You're a Drumstick Lipstick,
You're de foist
In da Irish Svipstick.
I'm a frightened frog
That can find no log
To hop,
But if, baby, I'm the bottom
You're the top!

All Through the Night

From "Anything Goes"

Words and Music by
COLE PORTER

93

94

BLOW, GABRIEL, BLOW
From "Anything Goes"

Words and Music by
COLE PORTER

heard you blowin' on your horn once more, So I said, "Sa - tan, fare - well"___

___ And now I'm all___ read - y to fly,_____ Yes to fly___ high-

- - - er and high - er!_____ 'Cause I've gone___ through brim - stone___

___ and I've been thru the fire,_____ And I've purged my soul And my heart too, So

BUDDIE, BEWARE

Published November 1934. Introduced by Ethel Merman.
Dropped after the New York opening and replaced
by a reprise of "I Get a Kick Out of You" by the week
of December 10, 1934.

VERSE

Since I know such a lot of men
The opinions that I've got of men
Are respected not only by amateurs but by pros.
I'd like to write a book on men
And explain that certain look on men
Which means they're about to propose.
Of course it helps a maiden's pride to be
In the class of somebody's bride-to-be
And the reason that I've escaped this doubtful
   bliss
Is because a certain fear in me
Wakes the honest pioneer in me
And instead of answering "Yes," I always say
   this:

REFRAIN 1

Buddie, beware,
Buddie, better take care,
Though at heart I'm a pearl
I'm a difficult girl,
So, Buddie, beware.
When I go to a show
I prefer the first row,
When invited to dine
I can't eat without wine,
So, Buddie, beware.
During Christmas holidays
I develop taking ways
And I'm not at all anti
Pretty things Santy
Brings from Cartier's.
Your devotion I prize
But you must realize, my boy,
Other girls' luxuries
Are my necessities,
So, Buddie, beware.

REFRAIN 2

Buddie, beware,
Buddie, better take care,
Even angels, I'm told,
Are still harping on gold,
So, Buddie, beware.
Somehow I don't feel nice
When I wear a dress twice,
Since the day I was weaned
I'm a caviar fiend,
So, Buddie, beware.
Now and then I like to see
Willie Stewart and Company
'Cause I hear divine voices
When their Rolls-Royces
Come and honk for me.
But if still you insist
And we riddle love's mysteries,
I should hate leaving you
For Wooley Donahue,
But, Buddie, Beware.

REFRAIN 3

Buddie, beware,
Buddie, better take care,
I must warn you that I'm
Simply never on time,
So, Buddie, beware.
When you order a steak
And no supper I'll take,
If you tell me I'm rude
When I play with your food,
Then, Buddie, beware.
I feel I should put you right.
As I lie in bed at night
While the twinkling stars gleam on,
With my cold cream on
I'm a lovely sight.
And another thing too,
When I'm married to you, my sweet,
If to come home you fail,
I'll open all your mail,
So, Buddie, beware.

BUDDIE BEWARE

From "Anything Goes"

Words and Music by
COLE PORTER

Since I know such a lot of men, The o - pin - ions that I've got of men Are re - spect - ed not on - ly by am - a - teurs but by pros. I should

like to write a book on men And ex - plain that cer - tain look on men Which
means _____ they're a - bout to pro - pose. Of course it
helps a maid - en's pride to be In the class of some - bod - y's bride - to - be. But the
rea - son that I've es - caped this doubt - ful bliss Is be -

(Guitar Tacet)

cause a cer-tain fear in me wakes the hon-est pi-o-neer in me And, in-

stead of an-swer-ing yes, I al-ways say this:

Andante (*very slow*)

Refrain

Bud-die be-ware, _____ bud-die bet-ter take care,_

Tho' at heart I'm a pearl,_

ANYTHING GOES
From "Anything Goes"

Words and Music by
COLE PORTER

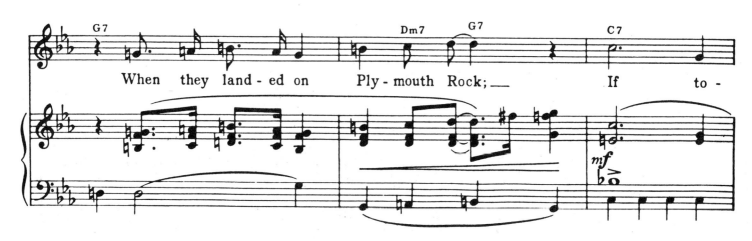

day _____ An - y shock they should try to stem, ___

'Stead of land-ing on Ply-mouth Rock, Ply-mouth Rock would land on them. __

REFRAIN

In old - en days a glimpse of stock-ing Was looked on as some-thing shock-

ing, Now heav - en knows, _____ An - y - thing goes. _____

ANYTHING GOES

Published November 1934. Introduced by Ethel Merman and ensemble. The lyric for an earlier verison of the first refrain was found in a copyist ink score at Warner Brothers Music warehouse, Secaucus, New Jersey, February 1982. Over the years Porter revised the sequence of the song's three refrains. Presumably, his final thougts are set down in the version published in *The Cole Porter Song Book* (1959).

VERSE

Times have changed
And we've often rewound the clock
Since the Puritans got a shock
When they landed on Plymouth Rock.
If today
Any shock they should try to stem,
'Stead of landing on Plymouth Rock,
Plymouth Rock would land on them.

REFRAIN 1

In olden days, a glimpse of stocking
Was looked on as something shocking,
But now, God knows,
Anything goes.
Good authors too who once knew better words
Now only use four-letter words
Writing prose,
Anything goes.
If driving fast cars you like,
If low bars you like,
If old hymns you like,
If bare limbs you like,
If Mae West you like,
Or me undressed you like,
Why, nobody will oppose.
When ev'ry night, the set that's smart is in-
Truding in nudist parties in
Studios,
Anything goes.

REFRAIN 2

When Missus Ned McLean (God bless her)
Can get Russian reds to "yes" her,
Then I suppose
Anything goes.
When Rockefeller still can hoard en-
Ough money to let Max Gordon
Produce his shows,
Anything goes.
The world has gone mad today
And good's bad today,
And black's white today,
And day's night today,
And that gent today
You gave a cent today
Once had several châteaux.
When folks who still can ride in jitneys
Find out Vanderbilts and Whitneys
Lack baby clo'es,
Anything goes.

REFRAIN 3

If Sam Goldwyn can with great conviction
Instruct Anna Sten in diction,
Then Anna shows
Anything goes.
When you hear that Lady Mendl standing up
Now turns a handspring landing up-
On her toes,
Anything goes.
Just think of those shocks you've got
And those knocks you've got
And those blues you've got
From the news you've got
And those pains you've got
(If any brains you've got)
From those little radios.
So Missus R., with all her trimmin's,
Can broadcast a bed from Simmons
'Cause Franklin knows
Anything goes.

Earlier version of first refrain

In former times a glimpse of stocking
Was looked on as something shocking,
But now God knows—
Anything goes.
Novelists who once knew better words
Now only use four letter words for their
  prose—
Anything Goes.
If saying your pr'yers you like,
If green pears you like,
If old chairs you like,
If backstairs you like,
If love affairs you like
With young bears you like,
Why, nobody will oppose.
And every night the set that's smart is
Indulging in nudist parties in studios,
Anything Goes.

THANK YOU SO MUCH MISSUS LOWSBOROUGH-GOODBY

Words and Music by
COLE PORTER

114

end by an-swer-ing "Yes." When I left Mis-sus Lows-bor-ough-

Good-by's,___ The let-ter I wrote was po - lite;___ But it

would have been bliss, Had I dared write her this, The let-ter I want-ed to write:

Thank you so much Mis-sus Lows-bor-ough-Good - by, Thank you so much,

Thank you so much for that in-fi-nite week-end with you. Thank you a lot, Mis-sus Lows-bor-ough-Good-by, thank you a lot; And don't be sur-prised if you sud-den-ly should be qui-et-ly shot For the

116

MISS OTIS REGRETS
(She's Unable To Lunch Today)
From "Hi Diddle Diddle"

Words and Music by
COLE PORTER

BEGIN THE BEGUINE

From "Jubilee"

Words and Music by
COLE PORTER

Spanish Version By
MARIA GREVER

123

WHY SHOULDN'T I?

From "Jubilee"

Words and Music by
COLE PORTER

stud-ied love dis-creet-ly, But now that I'm com-plete-ly free, I must

find some kind per-son-a gra-ta To give me

da-ta per-son-al-ly.

REFRAIN *Slowly, with tender expression*

Why should-n't I take a chance when ro-mance pass-es by,

sure when day is done, That the hour is com-ing when You'll be

kissed and then_ You'll be kissed a-gain,_ All de-bu-tantes say it's

good,_ And ev-'ry star out in far Hol-ly-wood Seems to give it a try, So

why should-n't I?_____ I?_____

JUST ONE OF THOSE THINGS
From "Jubilee"

Words and Music by
COLE PORTER

REFRAIN

EASY TO LOVE
From "Born To Dance"

Words and Music by
COLE PORTER

I'm sure you hate to hear_____ That I a - dore you, dear, But

grant me, just the same, ___ I'm not en - tire - ly to blame, For

Refrain *(slowly, with much expression)*

You'd be so eas - y to love, So eas - y to i - dol - ize, all

oth - ers a - bove, So worth the yearn - ing for, ____

Am7 D7 Bm C dim. Am
So swell to keep ev-'ry home-fire burn - ing for, We'd
Dm Am D7 G A#dim. G Am G
be so grand at the game, So care - free to - geth-er, that it does seem a
E7 Am Cm6 G A#dim. B7
shame, That you can't see Your fu - ture with me, 'Cause you'd be
Am7 D7 1. G D7 G Fdim. 2. G D7 G
oh, so eas - y to love! love!
mf
p

I'VE GOT YOU UNDER MY SKIN
From "Born To Dance"

Words and Music by
COLE PORTER

IT'S DE-LOVELY
From "Red, Hot and Blue"

Words and Music by
COLE PORTER

HE: I feel a sud - den urge to sing,— The kind of dit - ty that in-

vokes the Spring, So con - trol your de - sire to curse while I cru - ci - fy the

✿ Pronounced "delukes".

RIDIN' HIGH
From "Red, Hot And Blue"

Words and Music by
COLE PORTER

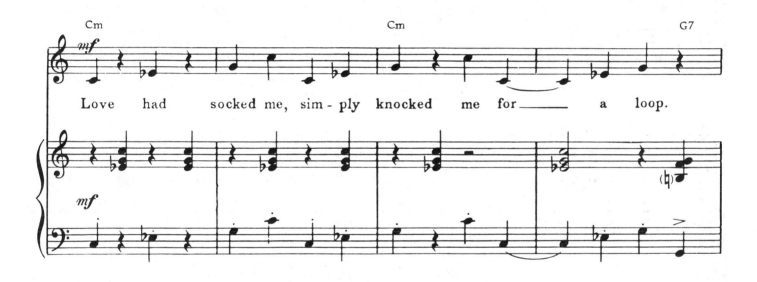

Love had socked me, sim-ply knocked me for _____ a loop.

Luck has dished me Till you fished me from _____ the soup.

150

151

IN THE STILL OF THE NIGHT
From "Rosalie"

Words and Music by
COLE PORTER

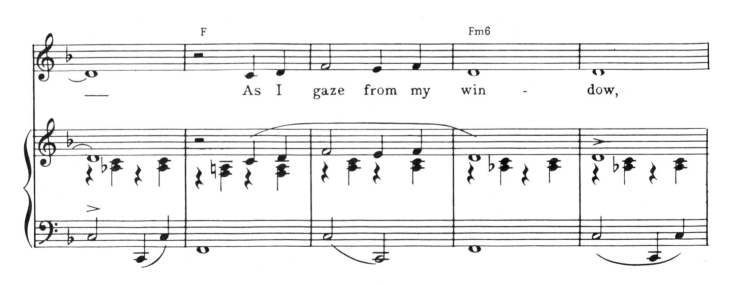

154

155

MY HEART BELONGS TO DADDY
From "Leave It To Me"

Words and Music by
COLE PORTER

MY HEART BELONGS TO DADDY

Published November 1938. This number launched the Broadway career of Mary Martin.

VERSE

I used to fall
In love with all
Those boys who maul
Refined ladies.
But now I tell
Each young gazelle
To go to Hell—
I mean, Hades,
For since I've come to care
For such a sweet millionaire.

REFRAIN 1

While tearing off
A game of golf
I may make a play for the caddy.
But when I do
I don't follow through
'Cause my heart belongs to Daddy.
If I invite
A boy, some night,
To dine on my fine finnan haddie,
I just adore
His asking for more,
But my heart belongs to Daddy.
Yes, my heart belongs to Daddy,
So I simply couldn't be bad.
Yes, my heart belongs to Daddy,
Da-da, da-da-da, da-da-da, dad!
So I want to warn you, laddie,
Tho' I know you're perfectly swell,
That my heart belongs to Daddy
'Cause my Daddy, he treats me so well.
He treats it and treats it,
And then he repeats it,
Yes, Daddy, he treats it so well.

REFRAIN 2

Saint Patrick's Day,
Although I may
Be seen wearing green with a paddy,
I'm always sharp
When playing the harp,
'Cause my heart belongs to Daddy.
Though other dames
At football games
May long for a strong undergraddy,
I never dream
Of making the team
'Cause my heart belongs to Daddy.
Yes, my heart belongs to Daddy,
So I simply couldn't be bad.
Yes, my heart belongs to Daddy,
Da-da, da-da-da, da-da-da, dad!
So I want to warn you, laddie,
Tho' I simply hate to be frank,
That I can't be mean to Daddy
'Cause my Da-da-da-daddy might spare
In matters artistic
He's not modernistic
So Da-da-da-daddy might spank.

DO I LOVE YOU
From "Dubarry Was A Lady"

Words and Music by
COLE PORTER

I CONCENTRATE ON YOU
From "Broadway Melody Of 1940"

Words and Music by
COLE PORTER

DREAM DANCING
From "You'll Never Get Rich"

Words and Music by
COLE PORTER

YOU'D BE SO NICE TO COME HOME TO
From "Something To Shout About"

Words and Music by
COLE PORTER

I LOVE YOU
From "Mexican Hayride"

Words and Music by
COLE PORTER

DON'T FENCE ME IN
From "Hollywood Canteen"

Words and Music by
COLE PORTER

BE A CLOWN
From "The Pirate"

Words and Music by
COLE PORTER

I'll re - mem - ber for - ev - er, when I was but three, Ma - ma, who was

clev - er re - mark-ing to me: "If, son, when you're grown up, you

want ev - 'ry-thing nice, I've got your fu-ture sewn up if you take this ad-vice:_

189

SO IN LOVE
From "Kiss Me Kate"

Words and Music by
COLE PORTER

FROM THIS MOMENT ON

From "Kiss Me Kate"

Words and Music by
COLE PORTER

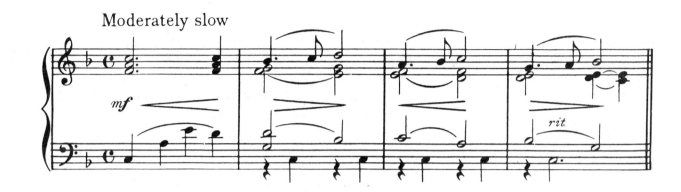

196

IT'S ALL RIGHT WITH ME
From "Can-Can"

Words and Music by
COLE PORTER

204

I LOVE PARIS
From "Can-Can"

Words and Music by
COLE PORTER

Moderato

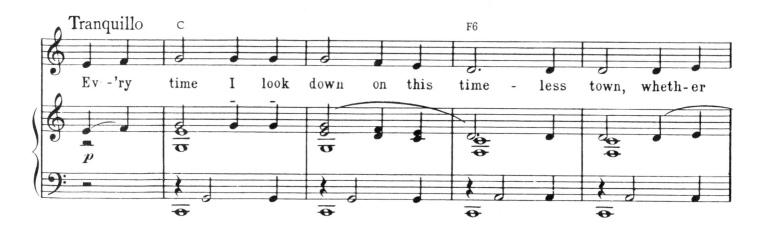

Tranquillo

Ev-'ry time I look down on this time - less town, wheth-er

blue or grey be her skies, Wheth-er

loud be her cheers, or wheth-er soft be her tears, more and

C'EST MAGNIFIQUE

From "Can-Can"

Words and Music by
COLE PORTER

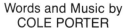

*Pronounced "say man-yee-fee-kuh"

ALL OF YOU
From "Silk Stockings"

Words and Music by
COLE PORTER

Fox trot tempo

(with bounce, but not too fast)

Af - ter watch - ing her ap - peal from ev - 'ry an - gle,

There's a big ro - man - tic deal I've got to wan - gle.

For I've fal - len for a

Refrain-Slowly

YOU'RE SENSATIONAL
From "High Society"

Words and Music by
COLE PORTER

He: A thor-ough know-ledge I've got a-bout girls, I've been a round__
She: A thor-ough know-ledge I've got a-bout boys, I've been a round__

And af-ter learn-ing a lot a-bout__ girls,
And af-ter learn-ing a lot a-bout__ boys,

This is the im-port-ant fact I found:
This is the im-port-ant fact I found:

220

TRUE LOVE
From "High Society"

Words and Music by
COLE PORTER